Be You, Get Noticed, Get Hired, Graduate CV

Susan Burke

SUSAN BURKE

A bit about Susan Burke

Susan Burke is an award winning careers consultant and coach. She is passionate about providing careers advice to young people and, as well as winning the Career Aspiration 2013 for the organisation she worked for at the time she also reached the finals in the UK Career Development Awards in the same year. She was also highly commended in 2012 by the National Careers Award for "Innovative Approaches to Working with Students in Education" from The Institute of Career Guidance.

Susan has been elected to the UK council for the Career Development Institute, representing career advice for young people and has written for many national newspapers. She also works as an Associate for The Career Transition Partnership, providing career advice to military personnel of all ranks leaving the Armed Forces.

Her website www.susanburkecareers.com has won two awards and she also provides training to other professional careers advisers in CV compilation and social media job searches. You can find out more about her through her website www.susanburkecareers.com.

Don't miss the Susan Burke Careers course that accompanies this book *The 90 Day Career Kick Start; How to make your degree worth it!* (http://susanburkecareers.co.uk/90-day-career-kick-start) and join her free private *CV Challenge Facebook Group* (http://j.mp/7DayCVResumeChallenge for more great tips and additional support.

Additionally with Sue's help you can learn to leverage your opportunities on LinkedIn so that potential employers are seeking you out – not the other way around! This is your opportunity to be seen; to start business networking and get yourself hired! Take a look now at Susan Burke's *LinkedIn Success Academy: Learn how to NEVER apply for Job Again!*
(http://linkedinsuccessacademy.com)

Other books by Susan Burke

Is your degree worth it? Learn the secrets of successful graduates...

(Coming soon – will be available February 2015) - *You can register for free here - to get this book as soon as it's published!* (http://j.mp/mydegreeworthit)

Having that hard-earned degree is definitely a positive when it comes to pursuing your chosen career, but it isn't enough. You need to make your degree financially worth it as you're paying a minimum of £9k in tuition fees each year, (not to mention living expenses), and it needs to pay you back tenfold.

I would love to teach you how to make your degree count so that you can get ahead FAST, and get that graduate job before you even leave university! You need to get business savvy and this ideally needs to start from day 1 of your university course, but trust me it's all still relevant in year 3, if you've not yet managed to secure that graduate job.

In this book we will look at how you view your career; goal setting to get you to where you need to be, and the 7 ultimate steps you need to take, to get yourself noticed and to ultimately get hired!

How this Book is going to help you to create that winning CV...

Hi my name is Sue and I am here to help you to get the job you want. However, before we begin I will need to be 100% honest with you: most CVs are rubbish! In fact, I will go as far as to say that most people don't even know what a good CV looks like, and CV shame is becoming a real problem!

Many CVs look exactly the same and most people make no effort whatsoever to differentiate themselves from other people, or to try to stand out from the crowd. This also brings YOU an amazing opportunity as if most CVs are bland, when a great CV hits the pile, it GETS NOTICED! This is what I intend to do for you. We are going to create a CV that's so great, every employer will be knocking down your door trying to find out more about you.

I promise you I'm serious about this and not just talk. The thing is, that most of us have never been taught how to compile a CV and if we have, it is probably just the generic route of picking up bits and pieces along the way and then trying to put it all together to form one document. Most of us are just stumbling along and not really thinking about how to get AHEAD or FAST TRACK ourselves. This is why I created this book, because I am tired of seeing graduates feeling that they are on the scrap heap, before they even enter the labour market.

I absolutely love 'Action Takers'. I love the people who 'DO' rather than 'SAY' and guess what, those are the types of clients that I work with day in and day out. They are the ones that get AHEAD.

My motto/catchphrase is: 'Live life on your terms'. and this is actively what this book will enable you to do. It will help you to get noticed and get HIRED. The real reason people don't get ahead is not because they don't know how to, but even when they do know and they have the information they need right in front of them, it's a fact that they often just don't act on it! I want you to be different so I've made this extremely simple for you. You can download my *free CV template*, (which I think you will love as it was created by an amazing graphic designer - https://sueburkecareers.leadpages.net/creative-cv). You can also check out *Appendix 1*, this is the CV framework that we are going to be using to create a killer CV. It will give you a guide to what we are going to be working on throughout the book and don't worry, I will be walking you through step by step with examples along the way, including the rookie mistakes that you're likely to make.

I am hoping that what will make this book different from any other that you will have read, is that it will stir you into ACTION when you see how simple it can be. You don't need to be a genius, all you need is common sense and to follow the 7 basic steps.

Just do it. No putting it off for another day. I've heard so many excuses in my time, boring...if you really think you've got what it takes and I know you have, because you're reading this now, then this is my personal invite to pop over to my free private *Facebook Group* (http://j.mp/7DayCVResumeChallenge). This is where you will receive additional support and get to meet students from all over the world who are also taking part. Feel free to ask any questions, and let's take the first step to getting you AHEAD!

Bury any past advice that you've received and burn (not literally) your generic CVs – it's time to get savvy and show employers what you're really made of.

Let's get started on creating your knock-out CV, be ready to invest just 15 minutes for each step. That's less than 2 hours of your life and once you have learnt these skills, you will have them forever!

This is not a generic CV Builder, it is personal advice from me because having spent my life as a Careers Adviser. I've seen hundreds of CVs over the years and not many that really inspired me! There is no right or wrong way to compile a CV, a CV works if it lands you an interview and mine always has.

So, welcome to the book that is potentially going to change your life by impacting how much you can earn! Dramatic statement perhaps, but if you follow the clear and concise advice contained within, I promise, the career you want can become a reality! If you need a little more TLC in approaching companies and want to learn "*How to get a job in a day*" check out my webinar, (fancy name for an online video –
http://susanburkecareers.co.uk/shop/how-to-get-a-job-in-a-day).

Before we do anything, please take a look at the two small tasks below…

1) What is your digital footprint?

Firstly, I would like you check out YOU! Go on, Google yourself! What have you found, were you surprised? So might your future employer be, if you do not have a squeaky clean profile!

Let this be a warning, most employers and recruiters do use the internet as a first port of call when checking out potential candidates, so you must make sure that they only ever find what you want them to see! Don't forget to check out Google images as well.

If it's the worst case scenario and you have found posts and images which are really not selling you, remove them immediately and untag yourself in photos. If this isn't possible, contact the website where any comments or images are being displayed and ask them to be removed. That said, it will also look highly suspicious if you have no online presence whatsoever and we will talk more about this later in the book.

2) Are you suffering from CV Shame?

Obviously in this book you are going to learn how to create a winning CV, however, are you wondering about the status of your current CV? Would it land you that dream job or would it more likely, end up in a recruiter's bin?

Imagine a way of being able to predict whether your CV is up to scratch or not. Envision not having to wait until you apply for a job to see if it actually measures up.

Wouldn't it be great to see if your CV is up to scratch right now before it gets to that late stage, or whether or not it needs a bit more loving and tender care?

Well don't fret! I have created a really quick survey of 14 multiple choice questions which will determine how much work you need to do. The survey is simple and best of all, it's completely free -and of course, if your CV does need a little work – I am here and on hand to help!

Take this quick free CV Appraisal (http://susanburkecareers.co.uk/dear-future-me/) to see if you are currently suffering from CV shame! If you are; don't panic, we will have you all sorted in no time at all!

Let's go! It all starts with Step 1.

Step 1 - How to create a winning CV

In this first chapter we will be looking at the overall picture. I will provide you with examples of what we are going to explore in further detail, later on. Think of the first chapter as an overview and a sneak preview of what you will need to be thinking about as you work your way through the book. Don't forget, you may want to refer to *Appendix 1* to get a feel for what we are going to achieve, it is a framework for creating a fantastic CV!

Why you need to work out your audience?

Before we even begin to create a CV, I would like to ask you what you intend to do with it? Are you going to upload it to job sites, or are you thinking about sending it directly to a hiring manager, or maybe you're looking to do both? Are you creating this CV with a particular job in mind, or are you creating this CV for a variety of different roles that you may wish to apply for?

This is really important as before we even start to create a CV, you need to know who your intended audience is. If you fail to understand the audience, your CV could end up being completely useless, which would be a huge shame because I want YOU to get the job, otherwise I would not have even entertained creating this book. What I do works and I want to prove it to you.

So let's discuss the questions I have just asked you! If you intend to use your CV to upload it to the various online job sites, then you need to understand how a CV is scanned and how to format it. A CV that will be uploaded to a job site will need to be less creative than something you would send to a hiring manager, as there are limitations on the formats that you can use.

If you intend to use your CV to apply for a number of different types of jobs, for example, let's say you want to earn some extra cash whilst at university, your CV needs to be tweaked and amended to match the requirements for each position that you're applying for. E.g. If you are applying for two different jobs, one as a Retail Assistant and another as an Admin Assistant; the skills sets will be different and this needs to be reflected in the CVs that you create.

So, Rule No. 1 - amend and tweak your CV to suit the requirements of each individual position that you're applying for and Rule No. 2 - think about who will see your CV (who are your audience), and how it will be used, as this will define how you create your CV and the style that you choose.

How to write your CV if you are uploading to a Job Site (so it is actually read by a real person!)

By registering with such sites, you can be notified when vacancies matching your description arise. By uploading your CV to the various online databases, recruiters will be able to find you by searching on specific keywords, (which, assuming that you have done a good job of your CV), will identify your CV as matching the description that they are looking for. The search engine technology these days may be ground-breaking, but it is only as good as the information you put into it and cannot make guesses on your behalf.

To get the most out of using online job websites and CV databases, you need to understand how they work, and particularly, how recruiters use them. These are some of the things that you should consider:

1.   Key words

When you upload your CV to one of these job websites, much of the initial process is automated, without any interaction from human beings! Your CV is run through a parser (software that breaks down formatting) and scores your CV due to its relevance; so as mentioned in the last paragraph – if your CV does not contain the keywords that the recruiter is searching for – your CV will not be found.

By this stage, you will have carried out your research to identify which descriptive words recruiters are likely to search on for the role that you are looking for. However, it's never too late to add to or amend your CV if the keywords that you have used, are not the same words that the recruiters are searching on.

For example, if you're a web designer, you would want to ensure that words such as Joomla, WordPress and all of the other platforms that you have experience with, are included somewhere in your descriptive bullet points and job titles, where relevant.

Once you are face-to-face with a recruiter, he/she may very well like you and your CV, however, you may never get that opportunity if the keywords in your CV are not the same key words that he/she is looking for. This doesn't only apply to your skills, it will also apply to your job titles, qualifications, languages and locations – so you will need to think carefully about which keywords you have used throughout your CV.

2.   Acronyms

Do not use acronyms on your CV, although *you* understand what the initials stand for, not everybody else will, for example: DoE, which stands for Duke of Edinburgh. There is an exception to this rule, where an acronym is so well known that it is unlikely that somebody would not know what it meant. For example, if you are an IT person who specialises in Search Engine Optimisation – it would be silly not to include the term SEO as this is a commonly used phrase throughout business, and it is possible that it would be used to search upon. Just make sure that you include both description and acronym (e.g. SEO would be in brackets), so that you could be picked up on either search.

The same applies to keeping descriptions standardised and not using in-house terminology. For example, if you are a Customer Services Manager, state that you're a Customer Services Manager – not a Service Performance Manager, as it is highly unlikely that anybody will be searching for the latter. You can always run a search on the various job titles and see which searches are the most popular, by where you receive the most results.

3.   CV Database Registration Form

One of the key things that many people overlook is the CV registration form. When you upload your CV onto a job site, you are also asked to complete a short online form which will ask you for basic information such as your contact details, your skills, preferred location, qualification, salary expectations, preferred job title and a summary of the type of work you're looking for. Many people do not bother to fill this in properly as all of the information can be found on their CV. However, many recruiters will also run searches on this information as well, therefore it is essential that you follow all of the other CV tips and rules regarding key words, acronyms etc. when completing the form.

4.   Regular Updates

If you've been looking for a job for a while, make sure you go back regularly and update or refresh your CV and re-submit it to whichever job websites that you are registered with. It's not uncommon for recruiters to only search the more recently submitted CVs on a website, believing them to be more up-to-date and therefore, more likely that the candidates will still be looking for work. So if your CV was last uploaded six months ago, it may be worth updating and re-submitting it. Your CV and registration form information should always be kept up-to-date, so if you develop new skills, take part in some volunteer or part-time work, or find an internship, make sure that your CV reflects this.

5. Design

I spoke to Employment for Students (E4S) to ask what they advise when students upload CVs to their job site. Chris Eccles states "most job boards parse (read and store plain text) CVs to allow employers to search them, they therefore only accepts CV's in a certain file types.

E4S is a student job board that accepts CV's as text, rich text, word or pdf files, which is standard across most mainstream job boards. CV parsing tends to struggle with heavily formatted CVs, so it is best to keep the layout fairly simple when uploading your CV to a job board. Also look out for maximum file sizes ranging from 200kb to 500kb. Including images and heavy formatting, increase the file size, so compress images before inserting them and don't go bananas with your CV design!

Later in this chapter, I will encourage you to do some 'blue sky thinking' when it comes to creating your own website and online portfolios. However, when uploading to job websites, they generally have a fairly strict format policy and if you have done anything too 'wacky' to your CV, it may not retain its formatting once uploaded. Although you are free to do what you want to grab people's attention by pointing them to somewhere else to find out more about you, avoid adding photos, patterns, graphics, text boxes and multi-column layouts and fancy backgrounds to any CVs that you are uploading to these particular websites and databases. The last thing you want is to get your CV in front of a recruiter and for him or her to not like your patterned borders, or for your boxes to be all wonky!

Find out more about Employment 4 Students

How to create your CV if you send direct to the Hiring Manager

Now if you are sending your CV directly to the hiring manager, the design can be what you want it to be, (as long as you think you've understood your audience, that is). You're free to download my *Creative CV Template* (https://sueburkecareers.leadpages.net/creative-cv) but remember this is not an advisable format for uploading to a job site, for the reasons explained above. You may also wish to explore my *CV Store* (http://susanburkecareers.co.uk/shop/cv-store) for other creative designs.

I'm going to teach you how to create a winning CV that I guarantee will get you that interview. I'm going to prove to you that it's actually easier than you think, and teach you about some of the common mistakes that students make when compiling their CVs.

In Step 1 – before you even put pen to paper; we are going to be looking at your CV and thinking about how we can make it absolutely amazing! We are going to use that time to brainstorm and get our ideas together. As mentioned previously, the vast majority of CVs out there are naff which presents you with a fantastic opportunity here, to put yourself head and shoulders above the rest.

I'm going to promise you now, that if you follow my step-by-step instructions, it will get you noticed and it WILL land you that interview. I know it's a big promise! You will need to follow every single step, regardless of whether you think it's relevant or not, and you're just going to have to trust me on this! It's not going to take an incredible amount of time, but the time that it does take, will make a huge difference to your CV and the way it's perceived.

Many people believe that there's a set formula that you must follow with regards to compiling a CV; that it must include something here, there, and be formatted in a particular way.

Now I'm going to tell you, there's no 'right way' with regards to compiling a CV. A CV works if it gets you that job. That's important. There are always two parts to a CV, the factual information and the subjective information.

The factual information is relatively easy to complete as it covers things such as, where you live, what school that you went to, the qualifications you obtained and any employment history or work experience. Where people get stuck is when they've got to talk about the subjective information such as 'Why do I want this job?'; 'What are my skills and abilities; how much relevant experience do I have? and how can I relate it to the position that I want to apply for?'

Well don't worry, we're going to cover all of this and I'm going to make it incredibly easy for you!

What I would like you to do now is to think as an employer would think, when you're creating your CV. I want you to really get into their mind set and I want you to think about: "What would an employer want to see in my CV?"

Think about the key things that you absolutely have to include, and whether the skills and experience displayed on your current CV match up to the skills set and experiences that an employer is looking for? Far too often when I see people's CVs, they are way too generic. Your CV MUST be matched to the skills and experience detailed in the job description that you're applying for, and likewise you need to remove any skills or qualities that are really not relevant to the role.

The vast majority of the time, you will be supplied with a job description of some sort for the position that you're applying for, however, if for any reason you don't receive a description of the role – simply Google the job title or type of job and you will see other descriptions that you can gauge yourself against.

So don't worry if you're not quite there yet. It doesn't matter, because over the next few chapters, I'm going to walk you through what you need to do.

In order to match your skills and experience on your CV to the kind of roles that you want to apply for, it is incredibly important that you do your research. If you do your research now, I guarantee that you're going to end up with a CV that has the 'WOW' factor! You want employers to look at your CV and to be able to instantly see that you are the perfect employee for this job, and that you have all of the skills and experience that they are looking for.

So whichever type of role it is that you're looking for; maybe it's as a Human Resources Assistant, an Events Manager, or something more scientific - check out the various online job vacancies and get an understanding for what that job is actually all about and what it involves. This will give you a great insight into what the employer is actually looking for in a candidate.

Now, I'm going to teach you a sneaky way to find out that information quite easily. I'm going to show you the *National Careers Service website* (https://nationalcareersservice.direct.gov.uk/Pages/Home.aspx). Look it up in Google and you will see that they have a section called, 'Job Profiles'. This *page*

(https://nationalcareersservice.direct.gov.uk/advice/planning/jobfamily/
Pages/default.aspx) gives us information on all of the skills and
requirements for any particular job. If you would like step-by-step
instructions on exactly how you can do this, check out *Video 1*
(http://j.mp/HowYouCanDoThis) by joining the *7 Day CV Challenge*
(http://7daycvchallenge.com).

Now this is not going to be a copy and paste exercise, each quality
needs to be personalised by you, but it is going to give you that
insight that you need when thinking about how to create your
winning CV.

So I now want you to think: "What is the job about?", "What skills
and experience do I need in order to be able to do the job?", "Can I
prove that I have them?" "What kind of evidence can I provide to
show that I've got what it takes, to get this role?"

Don't just list these things without actually backing it up, make it
quantifiable if you can.   You need to provide statistics where
possible for example, "I increased customer services satisfaction
by 10%, by following up with all customers when I said I would,
and at a time convenient to them", or "I reduced computer errors
by 5% by double checking all data entries". If you're telling me
that you've got excellent organisational skills, how did you obtain
them, how can you prove that you have them in your CV? I'm not
after a paragraph, just a precise sentence that will 'wow' me and
make me think, "I could really use somebody like that within my
organisation".

Think about how you improved the way the business ran and what
you did to achieve that? It is worth thinking about this now, as
these or similar types of questions also often pop up in interviews,
so it's great preparation for the big day!

Now, this is where it starts to become a little bit more interesting. I
want you to be a little bit creative. Obviously there are some roles

that you can be more creative with than others. However, on a serious note, I'm going to give you a few ideas to get you thinking along the right lines.

I want you to start thinking about what you can do to your CV to make it...well, more yours. Everybody can do something here and this is what's going to set you apart from any other candidate. However, I do want you to use some common sense, make sure that you think about your audience, think about the employer's mind-set and not your own mind-set. What are the employers looking to see in that perfect CV?

Incorporate Blue Sky thinking to get your CV Noticed & You Hired

So to get you started I'm going to get you thinking big! I like to call it 'blue sky thinking'.

Firstly, I would like you to do a search on Google; type in 'creative CVs' and also check out my *CV Shop* (http://susanburkecareers.co.uk/shop) for examples as well. It will be quite an eye-opener in terms of what you find, and not every design is going to be right for everybody, I just want you to understand what's out there in the marketplace right now.

I would also like you to check out the following two CVs, these are quite high-level Blue Sky thinking:

www.dearlisarudgers.com - this website went viral! This girl was looking for a Social Media Director position, so she created this website and believe it or not, she didn't get the job. However, she was offered another great job elsewhere. So, by creating this website, she brought the job offers directly to her, not the other way around!

www.cssdesignawards.com/sites/robby-leonardi/23615 - Robby Leonardi is a multi-disciplinary designer based in New York City. He works in illustration, graphic design, animation, and front-end development. He became famous in one sense, when his CV went viral, so check out his website www.rleonardi.com and I am sure you will be able to see how this little stunt, helped him to secure more projects from major media companies such as Fox, Speed TV etc.

Now these two CVs are admittedly quite high-end and this kind of design is not going to be suitable for everybody and the jobs that they are applying for. That's fine.

So let's bring this down to our level now, we can also use blue sky thinking in another way.

So, if you have a Twitter account (that's a professional account, please do not use a personal one - unless you think it's suitable), then you could perhaps incorporate this into your CV. Additionally, if you have a LinkedIn profile, this should also be added. Make sure you add your personalised LinkedIn URL, and if you've got a portfolio of work; you can of course also include a link to it in your CV.

If you are not yet on LinkedIn – you really should be, as you are missing out on valuable job opportunities. Perhaps you have previously caved in, having received one too many invitations and have actually joined the site, diligently setting up a barely-there account with a profile image and basic information and then left it at that? If that is the case, not only could you be missing out on a lot of lucrative opportunities, but even worse, you could actually be putting off potential employers.
LinkedIn has 300 million plus users and it is absolutely crucial that you have a really super profile that shows you off at your best – this is a real opportunity to sell yourself. If you need a little more

help why don't you join my *LinkedIn Success Academy: Learn how to NEVER apply for Job Again!* (http://linkedinsuccessacademy.com) and I can show you how to really make the most of this amazing platform and get yourself hired.

So, to summarise, everybody can add some colour. Maybe you've got a blog, or some other social media platform such as Pinterest- you can include these if they're applicable to the role that you're applying for. Pinterest, for example is great for those visual or creative roles such as graphic designer, architect, fashion or product designer, to name but a few.

You can even include quotes from people and testimonials, just try to think a little out of the box. Don't worry if you're unsure about any of this – we will dive into this topic in further detail, in another chapter 4. I just wanted to make you aware of your options, so that you can start getting your thinking cap on!

So to conclude the first step…

It's very important to understand that there is no set formula for writing a CV. Please believe me on this, it just comes down to whether it'll get you the job or not. So feel free to create your own style and formula.

Always keep in mind your audience-what is your employer looking for in your CV? How do your skills and experience match the job description?

Finally and last but not least; what can you do to set the scene, so that your CV creates the 'Wow' factor and stands out from the crowd?

So now it's over to you, I would like you to carry out the following tasks; (*now I know what you're thinking, I'll do this another time but you and I both know that time will never come, so you really must do it right now! I did promise you an amazing CV and this will actually take you much less time than you think it will!*)

Task 1 - Role, Skills & Qualities

Firstly, I would like you to identify the kind of skills and qualities that you think you have, and work out which are relevant in terms of the job that you are looking for by:

1. Visiting the following page of the *National Careers Service* (https://nationalcareersservice.direct.gov.uk/advice/planning/ jobfamily/Pages/default.aspx) to understand which skills, qualities and experiences employers require and look for in candidates for different types of roles. If you would like step-by-step instructions on exactly how you can do this, check out *Video 1* (http://j.mp/HowYouCanDoThis) by joining the *7 Day CV Challenge* (http://7daycvchallenge.com).

2. Have a think about which skills and qualities you already have, are looking to develop further and how you would prove that you are the right person for the role, (my checklist at the end of this chapter is pretty useful as it may help you to identify what you've been doing over the last 4 years) – also see task 2.

3. You need to understand which keywords apply to the particular roles that you wish to apply for. Look at how you would include them within your own CV and justify and backup your experiences and qualifications with evidence, (this is very important, particularly if you upload your CV to a jobsite as they will only scan for keywords – so if you have no key words

related to that job – guess what your CV may not even be read at all!)

4. As discussed previously, it is no good just adding the keywords to your CV, if in an interview you cannot provide proof of using that particular skill in a relevant circumstance.

So to summarise:

*   Look at various recruitment websites such as Indeed, Monster or E4S and academic job boards to understand what employers are looking for from potential candidates.
*   Think about which keywords need to be included in your CV?
*   How can you back this up with evidence?

Task 2 - What have you done in the last 4 years?

Ok, so whether you have been studying or working, (more so if you're a mature student); you will have something to contribute, and much to offer any organisation. Don't assume you've not done anything, because you will have, I can promise you this. Sometimes we tend to forget about the experiences we have had, why they matter and their importance in a working environment.

Many useful life skills and qualities are not gained in the workplace but can be applied there to very good use. For example, say you have completed your Duke of Edinburgh's award whilst still at school. In order to win this award you need to show strong survival skills; that you can work as a team and often as a leader in difficult and uncomfortable situations; that you can think on your feet when things don't go to plan and that you have shown initiative when having to find a different route or somebody lost the map! These are all great qualities which any employer would look for when taking on somebody to join their team.

The following list may help to jolt your memory and recall some of the experiences that you have had (some may now seem like a distant memory), and where you may have shown skills such as leadership, innovation, great organisational skills, dedication and commitment or excellent team work. You don't need to go back as far as your 5 metres swimming certificate, but you get my drift!

Below is a list of the types of activities that you may have taken part in – think about the skills and qualities that you learned from taking part in these activities. This is not a fully comprehensive list, it's just some ideas to get your mind working – can you think of any others?

Activities:

- Gap Year/ Months
- Erasmus Scheme
- Work Experience
- Taster Day
- Certificates / Achievements
- Job Shadowing
- Voluntary work
- Working on Committees
- Mentoring
- Clubs or Societies
- Duke of Edinburgh Award
- Football
- Netball
- Rugby
- Basically any type of sport
- Participating in Plays
- Debating Society
- Internship
- Travel
- Marathons
- Hill Walking

- Astronomy
- First Aid
- Fire Marshall
- Charity Work
- Sponsoring Events
- Magazine Committee
- Writer
- Blogs
- Conferences
- Professional Associations
- Relevant courses
- Industry related events
- Professional training in house
- Self-taught courses
- Languages
- Dance
- Gym
- Reading
- Horse Riding
- Skiing
- National Citizenship Service
- Prince's Trust

Hopefully Step 1 has set the scene and I look forward to taking you through the next chapter!

Step 2 - Creating your personal profile and statement

Welcome to Step 2. We're now going to start looking at how you can create your personal profile and how to be super clear and specify what you want, and what you are looking for.

Think about what we learnt from the last session and the importance we placed upon being creative. I want you to really think about that and about matching your CV to the job that you want. We also talked about how you must see your CV from the employer mind-set.

What is a personal statement?

A personal profile statement is a vital part of your CV and it is usually a short paragraph which gives an overview of the skills, quality and experience you have. Ideally, it should be placed just below your personal details i.e. your name, address etc.

The personal profile statement is the first thing that anybody reading your CV will see and tells the reader what sort of a person you are, so you need to be bold and confident and sell yourself to them in a positive way. This is your chance to get yourself noticed, so do it well, it is your own personal advert after all, but try not to go *too* over the top otherwise you may give off the appearance of being a little arrogant. Keep your statement relevant, positive, concise and to the point. The accepted length is around 5 or 6 lines. As with the rest of your CV, you will need to back up any skills and qualities that you say you have, with evidence.

Rookie mistakes you are likely to make when compiling your CV

As a careers advisor I see a lot of CVs, and I'm going to share with you some of the mistakes that people make. So here are some things to consider:

- Your email address - is it appropriate? Trust me, I've seen plenty which are not. Try and set up an email address which is fairly formal such as your firstname.surname@hotmail.co.uk as opposed to sexychick@hotmail.co.uk – you get the picture!

- Make sure you have the right contact details. Check and double-check. There is no point in sending your CV out if your telephone number or email address are incorrect, you will not get a response, it will also highlight your lack of attention to detail and rule you out of the game immediately!

- Do not include your National Insurance number on your CV if you're from the UK. This is a big no and apart from being a security issue, it is something that is only required once you start working with a company anyway.

- For me personally, I don't think you necessarily need to include the words 'Curriculum Vitae' or Résumé (if you're American). Surely it is obvious what it is, isn't it? However, again, it's purely your choice, there are no hard and fast rules surrounding this.

- And the final point I'm going to make is this: Make sure your CV is positive. Nothing on a CV should be negative. And if it can't be 100% positive, think about how you can put a positive spin on a negative event or just leave it off your CV altogether; although be careful about large gaps on your CV as you are likely to be questioned about them in an interview. Remember, a CV is your personal advertisement, so in an advert, we always try to only highlight the most positive bits!

So as a recap on Step 1 - when you first start out on your CV, you need to be looking at the factual information, (the easier bit!). So, that will cover your name, address, date of birth, contact details, employment history and work experience. It will also include any published articles, personal LinkedIn URL address and any other factual information that you would like a potential employer to see.

How to use your CV to divert people to want to find more about you

A CV should always be diverting people towards where they can find out more information about you, if they would like to, so you need to make this as simple as possible for them. In an ideal world, the best place to direct potential employers is your LinkedIn profile, as this is the platform that they are most likely to be familiar with, and it is a focal point where everything about you can be seen in one place. Remember, if you need help with your LinkedIn profile, please have a look at my *LinkedIn Success Academy: Learn how to NEVER apply for Job Again!* (http:// linkedinsuccessacademy.com) for more information on how to make yourself stand out from the crowd.

Now there are some rookie mistakes that we all tend to make, and I want to make them very clear so that you don't fall into the same trap!

- It's quite impressive how some people manage to do this, but try not to if you can help it; you can't condense several months of doing something really remarkable (such as volunteering for a charity), into one sentence. So if you've taken part in something that is really going to highlight your amazing qualities and skills, how can you expand on this? Reflect and think what skills and qualities you have obtained through your experience, what you've learnt, how this is relevant to an employer and how they can be transferred to within a workplace. Please do bear in mind though, that you do really need to keep your CV to a maximum of 2 pages as otherwise you may put people off wanting to read it if it's too long, and reads like War and Peace!

- When you start your personal profile, make that opening paragraph clear and concise but make it personal, humanise it and talk about you and what you have to offer.

- I'm going to explain more in a little bit about how to create a brilliant personal profile, but what you always need to keep in the back of your mind, is: 'What would make me want to read further?' Employers and recruiters receive hundreds of CVs on a daily basis (most of which get tossed straight into the bin), and you only have about 10 seconds to make an impression. You need to get it right!

So back to your personal profile. It really is all about you but do remember that an employer is not a mind-reader and they do not have a crystal ball. So I want you to spell out what you want from them. Are you looking for part-time, full-time work, an internship or work experience? Let them know, tell them in your CV. Make absolutely sure that you're clear on what you want to gain from this job. Remember, you need to work out what the role is and what it involves; what skills, qualities and experience is required, and how you can support and highlight what they are looking for in your personal profile.

So a personal profile is, in a sense, an overview of your whole CV. This means that you can mention things twice if need be. So you might want to mention something at the start in your profile, but at a later stage in your CV, you may (and probably should), want to add more meat and get into more detail.

I know that I do keep coming back to this but it really is so crucial! Think again about your key strengths and about what will impress an employer the most. Don't be shy and just remember you only have approximately 10 seconds to impress them!

Examples of personal profile statements

So, below are two examples of personal profiles that I would like us to go through and critique:

1) This is the personal profile of a 'want to be' writer:

"I'm a confident person with excellent communication skills. I'm also articulate and have shown that I'm extremely focused by always meeting tight deadlines, particularly with regard to coursework. My greatest strengths are my research and writing skills.

I am looking to achieve an internship as a trainee journalist. I have compiled several articles on student life which have all been published in the University Magazine "The Highest Degree". I have received numerous written compliments from teachers and students for the quality and content of my articles".

So firstly, what I love about this is that it's very clear. It is also backed up and evidenced. The person has shown that they are focused by managing to meet all of their deadlines. They've also received a number of written compliments from teachers and students on their content and article writing for the University Magazine, which speaks for itself. This is really great.

2) This is the personal profile of a trainee nurse:

"I am a loyal, talented and caring person who loves making a difference to the lives of the people that come into our hospital. I'm open-minded, patient and supportive towards other people, especially towards those under my care and who are sick. I've an excellent ability to remain unflappable under pressure".

Now, I have to admit that I really do not think that this is quantified enough. There is nothing to back up this person's statements, for example – they say that they are unflappable under pressure, but how have they proved that? This person should have said something along the lines of "I have proven that I'm unflappable under pressure because on this occasion, this happened.....and I reacted in this way..... Which meant that the issue was resolved calmly and everybody escaped unharmed".

Just an example but you can hopefully understand what I'm trying to say and what I'm trying to get out of you?

So, to conclude this step; the factual information of a CV, which is the basis, is super easy. The next bit, which is your personal profile and the more subjective part, takes a little bit more work.

So to conclude the second step:

- Don't assume an employer will know what you're looking for in a job. Be very clear on what you want.

- Any skills or qualities that you state in your CV MUST be backed up with evidence.

- Remember, you've only got those 10 seconds to really impress. How are you going to create the 'wow' factor and make them want to read more about you?

- Your personal profile is key and my advice is, don't be shy. Really sell yourself!

Creating your personal profile statement...

You have read how to create a personal profile with the 'wow' factor. The two examples that were shown are good, but you could improve on these and you will need to make it very clear to any potential employers what you are looking for (spell it out in the personal profile section). For example: 'I am looking for an internship' or 'I am seeking work experience'. Whatever it is you are looking for, make it very clear.

You will also earn extra brownie points if you can name the company in the CV, but be careful, pay attention and make sure that you amend the company name each time if sending your CV to multiple companies. Make absolutely sure that your CV **does** go to the company named on your Cover Letter and only **that** company, otherwise you won't get a look in! You have been warned!

An example in action... take a look here at *video 2* (http://j.mp/ HowYouCanDoThis) which shows a number of examples of personal profiles along with my critique.

Start thinking about how you can improve your own profile by personalising and bespoking it. Remember to list and justify any skills, qualities or relevant experience with backed-up evidence.

How to complete a CV if I lack work experience?

If you don't have the relevant experience for the job that you want, don't panic, have a think about your transferable skills and see how you could apply those skills in the new role. If you're unsure what transferable skills are, check out Chapter 3 - I am positive this will really help you.

The next step is to think about how you can gain relevant experience, and I hear you loud and clear – you're probably muttering "but this is why I am creating my CV in the first place". Point taken, however, you may find it easier to get some experience via voluntary work. Voluntary work is highly rated these days and there are many sites listing open opportunities. Do a Google search on voluntary work in your local area and see what is on offer, if you live in the UK, www.do-it.org.uk may be useful.

However, there is another way. Consider a job site similar to *Employment 4 Students* (http://www.e4s.co.uk), as they can even help students who don't have much work experience as they offer a range of part time and holiday jobs where training is either provided, or experience is not required. This includes jobs across a range of sectors including retail, sales, hospitality, administration, and even event stewarding at music concerts and major sporting events.

Tutoring jobs are ideal for students and recent graduates because they are flexible, often with evening or weekend hours, but pay extremely well at £15 - £30 per hour. Experience is a bonus, but not essential, and you only need A-Levels to be able to tutor kids taking exams up to GCSE level. Graduates can also tutor A-Level students and command a higher hourly wage.

Freelancing is another great option for students with little or no work experience. There are numerous freelancing websites which allow freelancers to bid for work projects from companies large and small around the world. Projects range from running a company's social media account to writing blog posts, creating a logo or other artwork, drafting legal contracts, or web development work. There are projects suitable for any student and you can build up a portfolio of work and testimonials which will add credibility to your CV. Tutoring and freelance work can be found on E4S.co.uk so maybe worth checking it out.

Step 3 - Match it!

How to make your CV targeted to the job you want

We're up to Step 3, and this chapter is called Match It! It's all about your skills and qualities.

Very soon, you will be able to match any required skills and qualities in any role, to your CV. Now I know we touched on this briefly in Step 1, but I thought it needed a little more explanation.

So just a quick recap on the last chapter. We talked about your personal profile and hopefully you can see that your profile is an overview, it's your advert and is all about you. We learnt that you need to be really super clear on what you want to achieve. So whether it's a graduate job, an internship or work experience; make sure you spell it out.

Continuing along that theme, we're going to look at the difference between a quality and a skill.

We need to understand the difference in order to write a compelling CV.

Why skills, qualities and transferable skills matter

A quality is a personal characteristic. It could be that you describe yourself as honest, reliable and hardworking, for example. A quality is often something that we are born with, part of our nature.

A skill is something you will have learnt, so it could be something like the fact that you are now a Social Media Guru, or great with IT or you've learnt how to play an instrument. It's maybe something that you have studied for, or you've taken part in a course in order to learn how to do something. It is important that we understand these differences as it makes it so much easier when we're talking about skills and qualities in relation to a CV.

So, let's get back to that employer mind-set. I want you to really, really think about what a potential employer or recruitment manager would want to see in your CV with regard to your skills and qualities, and how they would match up to that job.

I'm going to give you a tip. If you applied for a job as a Retail Assistant, and then perhaps six months later you applied for a job as a Finance Assistant; both CVs would need to be different because the related skills and qualities are obviously not the same. Your CV needs to be adapted every time you apply for a different type of role to match the requirements, skills and qualities needed for that particular job.

The next part to understand is; that we all have transferrable skills. Yes, every single one of us does. So, even if you're thinking "I don't think I do", you do and I'm going to give you a really simplistic way of looking at this.

Let's look at an example of a footballer, even if you don't play football, you will still get the gist of what I'm saying. The **qualities** you would develop from playing this sport include commitment and reliability (to turn up at every game and for practice), discipline, punctuality and learning how to be a team player, amongst other things. The **skills** that you would develop may include co-ordination, dribbling, shooting and scoring; all of these skills and qualities added together, would hopefully make you into a good football player. So we can see that there are different things that we're developing and that need to come together to complete the picture. Some of these skills and qualities are transferable to the workplace. If as a footballer in your free time, you were asked to provide an example of teamwork – you have one right here!

So why am I mentioning transferable skills? Well, do you remember in Step 1 - I suggested that you write down what you've been doing over the last 4 years in order to get an overall impression? Well, now you can see how this could be relevant to your CV. You may have skills and work experience that are directly relevant, or you may be able to use your transferable skills from the different activities you have taken part in, in a non-direct way.

How to make sure your CV is jargon free

A rookie mistake that is often made is when jargon is used that only certain people will understand.

For example, when I started working in a school as Head of Careers , I kept coming across the term "DoE". I kept asking myself, "What is DoE?", because it kept appearing on students' CVs, (it stands for the Duke of Edinburgh's Award – in case you were wondering!). These are the sort of acronyms and jargon words that unless you've actually taken part in this yourself, you are unlikely to know or understand. Now there is one exception and that is, that you can by all means use jargon that's related to the field or job that you are applying for. As long as you are sure that any potential employer will know what it stands for and what it means. If you are unsure, it's always best to spell it out!

So, the key lesson for this chapter is to make sure that you look thoroughly at the job profile for whichever position you are applying for. Take the time to study exactly what it is that company are looking for in a candidate, so that you can closely match your skills and qualities to their requirements.

Make sure that you go on to the National Careers Service website (https://nationalcareersservice.direct.gov.uk/Pages/Home.aspx). Take a look at the different job roles, where you will see a list of the key skills, qualities and experience that they are looking for. So if for example, you were interested in becoming an Events Manager, search on that job title and see what the specifications are. If you would like step-by-step instructions on exactly how you can do this, check out *Video 3* (http://j.mp/HowYouCanDoThis) by joining the *7 Day CV Challenge* (http://7daycvchallenge.com).

Once you have looked at what they require from you, (do not just copy and paste these into your CV!), start thinking, "Okay, these are the skills and qualities that they've specified they want to see. How can I demonstrate that I have those skills and relate them to the post that I want?" You need to make sure that when you do this, you keep it personal to you.

On your CV you should include just a couple of lines on each skill that you have chosen to highlight, however stick to no more than 4 or 5 skills and really build on those by providing strong evidence and concrete examples to justify why you think you have those attributes.

So let's put this into context. I'm going to show you two examples, which I really love:

Examples of skills and qualities used in a CV

This person has chosen **'organisation'** as one of their key skills to highlight on their CV.

"Whilst volunteering as a membership secretary for a local rugby club, I organised a successful recruitment drive, printing flyers, and organising other members of the club to distribute them

around their workplaces, clubs and schools. The flyers offered special discounts on club kit, and snacks and drinks in the club. I also organised an open day so that people could be shown around the club and try it out. Membership at our rugby club increased by 20% over a 6 week period"

I absolutely love this. Through this statement, they have not only been able to evidence their organisational skills, but they have also proved that they are efficient and effective as through their skills in organisation, they have increased membership by 20%.

Think about how you could create a powerful statement like this by implementing this technique. If you have any statistics – they are always great to throw into the mix as it proves that your campaign or project resulted in an increased turnover, subscription list, number of customers, sales etc. However, do not make up these figures if you do not have them, as you may be asked to give a more detailed account in interview!

In my second example, the candidate has chosen **'communication'** as his/her key ability.

"During my recent internship, I was asked to take part in some market research, interviewing members of the public regarding their opinions of a new food product that the company is thinking about adding to their range. I compiled the survey itself and after interviewing over 100 people, I presented my findings to a group of mixed level managers in a formal presentation. I was complimented on my presentation and public speaking skills, as well as my interesting and inspiring slideshow and hand-outs. I also received exemplary written feedback from my manager."

So not only has this person evidenced that they are great at communication, they've also provided a written endorsement from the previous manager as well.

These are two very good examples, but they're only good if the statement relates to the job that you're applying for. Remember that.

Task 1 - Skills and qualities

So now it's your turn. I want you to pick four of your own skills or qualities that relate to a job that you would like to apply for, (having first researched it on the National Careers Service website https://nationalcareersservice.direct.gov.uk/Pages/Home.aspx); and write a powerful and justified sentence/paragraph about each of them, including any statistics where you can.

For example; perhaps the first job that you're looking for as a graduate is as an Accountant:

You would need to pick (perhaps four) applicable keys skills and qualities so you may select:

- Mathematical & computer skills
- Analytic skills
- Report writing
- Accuracy and attention to detail

Then you would need to take each of the above skills and qualities and turn them into a powerful statement that demonstrates how and why you think you have that quality.

Please see the below example for how a person may illustrate their '**Analytical**' skills:

"During my Accountancy degree course, we were assigned a group project to take part in financial research for a local business. It turned out that I had the strongest analytical abilities in the group,

so I led in the analysis of the data that we collected. Due to my analytical skills, we were able to show the business where they needed to improve financially in order to increase their profitability."

Pick four key skills and qualities relevant to the position that you would like to apply for and think how you can create a powerful statement like the above, to demonstrate your talent!

Step 4 - Let's talk style!

Content maybe king but your CV needs to look good as well

This chapter is all about how we're going to structure your CV. A CV must have great content but it must look great as well, and this is often what's missing from most CVs.

We now know that we need to get into that employer mind-set, and hopefully that's now easier than you first thought. Recruiters have to read hundreds of CVs and I'm sure that after a while, one looks pretty much the same as another, so in order to make your CV stand out from the rest, we need to get creative!

For those that feel that they have no creativity whatsoever, have no fear – help is at hand! I would like to start by talking about the style. Employers really don't have a great deal of time, so you need to bear in mind that you probably only have a 10 to 30 second window to create a great first impression and make them want to keep on reading!

There are various rookie mistakes that are made when creating CVs, most of which I have seen being a careers advisor. The first is quite simply, too much information. Anything more than two pages is too long, anything shorter may not be enough. (an exception to this maybe if you are attending a jobs fair you may just provide a 1 page resume/CV) Remember, this is your chance to sell yourself, without boring them to death! So your CV needs to be concise, to the point and easy to read. If your CV is so crammed full of information that there is no white space available, employers will most probably not even look at it.

So the essence of this chapter is get you thinking about design, how are you going to set out your CV and make it pleasing to the eye? In order to do this, I need to get you thinking big picture and a little bit out of the box, I call this blue sky thinking.

How to get the hiring manager wanting to find more about you

I'm going to throw some things out there to try and inspire you and get your creative juices flowing.

Firstly, although you need to keep your CV to within 2 pages, there is nothing to say that you can't direct people to other places where you can expand on this information and display some of your work or more of your personal profile. So if you are a wannabe journalist you may direct people to your blog, if you're a designer to your portfolio.

People are curious by nature and if your CV is well written and structured, they will want to find out more about you. Another great way to do this is through a personal website, which is all about you and what you do. Your CV should also direct people to your LinkedIn profile - this really is a MUST.

Whilst we're on the subject, why not come and connect with me on *LinkedIn* (https://www.linkedin.com/in/susanburkecareers). I would love you to do so, but don't forget to let me know the reason why we are connecting, which is obviously through this book! Remember, that if you still need help creating a brilliant LinkedIn profile - that will really sell you, and best of all show you how to connect with hiring managers, why not join my *LinkedIn Success Academy: Learn how to NEVER apply for Job Again!*_(http://linkedinsuccessacademy.com), where I can show you how to really make the most of this amazing platform, and get yourself hired?

The formatting of a CV is something that I know people really struggle with, so to help you I have created some CV templates for you to use in my *CV/Resume Store* (http://susanburkecareers.co.uk/shop/cv-store). I created these templates as I was fed up of seeing average looking CV's and I wanted to show you what a good CV can look like. They are all word based documents, so you don't need any technical skills to use them but it will give you a basis to build from and really shine, so please check them out (http://susanburkecareers.co.uk/shop/cv-store).

How to use FREE online resource to build you as a brand

If you do think that you're up to the challenge of creating something amazing online to highlight your skills, I would like you to check out this fantastic website. It's completely free, and I'm going to show you how you can use it to your very best advantage. The website is called Flavors.me. If you click on the hyperlink and take a look, I'm going to give you an example of what it can do for you.

Flavors.me will help you to create a gorgeous, free website in minutes, so you can get yourself up and running quickly. However, remember, the whole reason that you are doing this is to enhance your CV. This website should be purely a place where you can advertise your best bits and where people can find out more about you.

I'm now going to show you an example of how this can play out. I strongly advise you to log on to my website (http://7daycvchallenge.com/login), so that I can show you examples of how people use other free resources to build themselves as a brand, please refer to Video 4 (http://j.mp/HowYouCanDoThis).

Ways to create your CV

There is another option. You may prefer to create a custom-made CV if you have the technical and IT skills to be able to do this. However, if not, you could also hire a freelancer to do it for you on *People Per Hour* (http://www.peopleperhour.com) or other such site. If you do hire somebody else to design your CV, you will still need to provide the content yourself. Don't let somebody else write about you as you know yourself better than anyone else.

If you are going to get somebody else to design your CV, make sure that you will be able to update it yourself, otherwise it will be of no use to you, as you will not be able to adapt it and personalise it for different job roles and as you move on. You will also need to make sure that you request all source files and remember to find out which software package they will be using and can you update it if necessary?

So you have created your CV template; you have created your personal website so what else could you do to make your CV stand out?

A fantastic testimonial on your CV will always impress. It should be honest and submitted by either a tutor, previous employer or from somewhere that you may have taken part in volunteer work, for example. You can direct people as to what you would like it to say, particularly if you want to highlight specific skills or qualities that may be relevant to a position that you're applying for. Whatever you do, don't get relatives to write a testimonial for you as you will lose credibility and it looks a bit desperate.

So now you really need to start seriously thinking about the layout of your CV. Which framework are you going to use? Some people write their CV in the third person, that's fine and there's nothing wrong with this and it really is your decision. However, personally,

I just feel that I own a CV more if it comes from me, as I'm able to get my personality across. People have different views on whether a CV should be written in the first or third person so there is not necessarily a right and wrong answer here, it comes down to personal choice.

Don't forget to add the visual links to your social media platform, personal website, or LinkedIn profile, or as we said earlier; maybe you've got your own portfolio or your own blog, these can all be linked and incorporated into your CV.

If you've not already done so, you may wish to download my own creative CV (https://sueburkecareers.leadpages.net/creative-cv), which you can use and update in Word.

Task 1 - Let's talk style!

- Your CV should not just contain great content, but should look good as well, so check out my CV Store (http://susanburkecareers.co.uk/shop/cv-store).
- Think about how you are going to set out your CV. Why not check out Video 4 (http://j.mp/HowYouCanDoThis) from the 7 Day CV Challenge?
- Check out my FREE CV Templates (http://susanburkecareers.co.uk/cv-templates/ - but the key is to customise the template to you).
- Work out if you are going to include social media platforms. Only use social media if it's applicable, (use caution), it needs to be professional and role related....
- Feel free to connect with me on LinkedIn (https://www.linkedin.com/in/susanburkecareers) and don't forget to let me know the reason why – this book!

Work out whether you will use:

- A CV Template - (check out my CV/Resume Store http://susanburkecareers.co.uk/shop/cv-store)
- Create your own
- Get someone else to do it for you - for example, through People Per Hour (http://www.peopleperhour.com)
- Maybe you also want to create your own website - check out flavors.me

Don't forget - you really should be on LinkedIn – and not just a 'barely there' profile, we are talking about a profile that actually 'SELLS' you 24/7.   Please see my *LinkedIn Success Academy: Learn how to NEVER apply for Job Again!* (http://linkedinsuccessacademy.com) for how to get noticed and how to get hired on LinkedIn.

Step 5 - Compiling your employment history...

Can you believe it, we're on Step 5, which means that we're over half the way there!

This chapter will explain the best way to compile and lay out your employment history and even if you don't have much work experience, I'm going to show you how to make the most of what you have.

So, just to recap on what we covered in the last step; we talked about the structure of your CV and why it's so important. Yes, content is obviously key, but if we can get the structure and design right and make the CV look great, we're making sure that your CV is absolutely going to grab that employer's attention.

Continuing with the next step, I'm going to ask you to use your logic and common sense. When compiling your work history, you must always start with the most recent and work backwards. As I said; it's just common sense really, any employer is going to be far more interested in what you have been doing over the last year or so, rather than what you were doing five years ago! This is really important, and the same principle also relates to qualifications, professional training, courses and the like.

Employment history obviously covers all of the work experience that you have gained. So it may be that you have completed an internship, taken part in volunteer work, gained some work experience through shadowing or had some part-time work whilst studying; or if you are a mature student, you may have a full employment history.

What to do if I don't have much work history?

If you feel that you don't have any work history, there's no need to panic. Often this is a chicken and egg situation, where you don't have work experience and so are finding it difficult to land a job, but if you can't get a job, how are you supposed to build up experience? If this is you, go back and refresh yourself on page 22 as this will help you to put a strategy together on how to make this happen. Don't forget your university is probably able to help as well, there is always lots of support available and this is definitely an area to explore.

How to set out your work history, without boring the Hiring Manager!

So let's start thinking about your work history, I'm going to make this incredibly simple to do. I would like you to take your last job and do the following:

- Provide two sentences of the general duties that you were responsible for in that job, to give an overall feel for what the position entailed.

- Give me three or four bullet points of your key achievements in that post if you can.

- Now quantify these achievements using statistics where possible, as discussed in previous chapters.

Don't use great big, long lists. Bullet points are best as they are more concise and easier to read.

We are now going to look at a couple of examples of extracts from CVs and how they could be improved upon. Now if you want to

see this in action, check out Video 5 (http://j.mp/
HowYouCanDoThis) to really get you started.

Practical examples of how to set out your work history in your CV

Work Experience

Sales Assistant, Boo Enterprises, Guildford, GU9 1XT
January 2013 – Present Date

Key achievements:

- Achieved four out of five revenue targets, equating to over 120% against overall targets set during entire period of employment
- Have personally invoiced over £20,000 since starting in role
- Demonstrated resilience and ability to up-sell products and consistently met Key Performance Indicators (KPIs) and objectives
- Significantly improved negotiation skills, regularly converting customers from point of enquiry to sale, which earned me an award for best Sales Assistant during the month of July

This CV belongs to a sales assistant. Now personally, I love the key achievements. However, the key duties are missing so that I can't get an overall feel for what the person is selling and what their position is: what does the role actually involve?

So to reiterate, you need to ensure that you always include key duties, and then key achievements.

The key achievements that have been listed are fantastic, there's nothing wrong with these. I'm going to give you two examples.

- Achieved four out of five revenue targets which equated to over 120% against overall targets set during the entire period of employment.

- Significantly improved negotiation skills. Regularly converted customers from the point of enquiry to sale; something which earned me the Sales Assistant of the period during the month of July.

So you can see, this is super because it's personalising and quantifying the statements with figures.

The next CV that we are going to look at is a CV for a bartender – On the next page, you can see an example of duties, which need to be listed on your CV for each job as well as the key achievements.

Employment History

Bartender, Laws Bar, Liverpool, L1 6FQ
April 2014 – Present Date

Duties:

My main duties are serving people in a friendly and polite manner and ensuring the bar is stocked at all times.

Key Achievements:

- Helped train new staff in key competencies and procedures.
- Demonstrated an in-depth knowledge of key health and safety standards.
- Achieved food hygiene certification.

Hopefully, I have now managed to get my message across but I am going to provide you with one more example:

2008 – Present, Store Manager, Costa Coffee, 31 High Street, Wimbledon, SW19 2DQ

Duties

- *My role is the daily management of the store, providing high quality service and managing a team of 20 staff.*

Key Achievements

- Increasing sales by 10% by analysing store figures and improving customer service as well as managing and motivating the team increase sales and ensure store efficiency.
- Reducing stock, waste and other store costs by 5% resulting in a saving of £7,000 per annum.
- Being able to motivate staff, reduce absenteeism by listening to my staff and to improve working conditions.
- Responsible for recruitment and team training provision to help new staff and more experienced staff excel.
- Highly competent to organise work schedules, track accounting and payroll to provide quarterly reports to the Regional Director.

Task 1 - Compiling your employment history

- Compile your own work history, and if possible, try to split this into duties and key achievements.

- Just to clarify, duties should just be just one or two sentences, to give a brief overview of the job.

- Your key achievements should be one to four bullet points of what you feel that you've achieved whilst in that post.

Step 6 - Joining it all together

Nearly there! This chapter is about how we join that CV together, so stay with me.

So let's just recap on what we learnt in the last chapter. We understand that your work history needs to be compiled of one or two sentences for each job, which generally just states your general role and what the position entailed. This is followed by concise bullet points setting out your key achievements or key outcomes for that post. This is what is going to make you stand out.

This chapter though, is all to do with training and qualifications, and our hobbies and interests. This can also come under the title of 'Additional Information' on your CV. We will also look at references.

How to set out your training and qualifications in your CV with detailed examples

So let's just focus on what I actually mean by training and education.

The obvious start would be to list your standard education at school and in college. We should also obviously add any university degrees in this section. The less obvious things that you may want to include in this section would be any professional training that you may have received. You may have taken part in some in-house training, or you may have volunteered with an organisation and they have supplied you with some training. You may have completed an online course on social media management or taught yourself how to use a particular software package. This can all go on our CV. If you have a full clean driving licence, this can also be included here.

As discussed previously when talking about employment history, the same applies to qualifications with regard to starting with the most recent and working backwards. There is a way of making this look really neat and succinct, and I'm going to show you how to do this. If you want to see this in action, take a look at Video 6 (http://j.mp/HowYouCanDoThis).

Weirfield School, Taunton, Somerset, TA1 5AY (Sep 2007 – Aug 2012)

GCSE	Grade	GCSE	Grade
Maths	A	History	B
English Literature	A	French	B
English Language	A	German	C
Biology	A	Information Technology	C
Chemistry	A	Art	C

I love this, and I'm going to tell you why.

We can see that this person studied A Levels and that they've placed their highest grades at the top with the lower grade at the bottom. You can also see that it's nicely aligned into a column, so that it's very easy on the eye and simple to read. Likewise, with the GCSE section, again the same thing, it's all neatly aligned, with the highest grade at the top and working down to the lowest grade.

Now I would like you to get into that mind-set. There is just one thing to bear in mind though: in the future, or perhaps even now, you could record these as simply: '(Nine) GCSEs Grades A-C, including Maths, English and Science'. This may be the case if many years have passed since taking those initial exams or just because you need to free up room on your CV, again, it's up to you.

EDUCATION/QUALIFICATIONS

Upper Chine School for Girls Shanklin, Isle of Wight P037 7LL (Sep 2012 – Present Date)

A Levels and predicted grade

Maths B*
Biology C*
Chemistry B*
Geography A*

The above example is what I don't like, maybe it's just me and perhaps I have a little OCD going on, I don't know. However, the reason that I wanted to show you this, is that the grades are not aligned and, as discussed before, Geography should be at the top as it's the highest grade. It's just not easy on the eye. Try to avoid this if you can, as it just doesn't look very good.

Below are very good examples of how a student has set out their educational university degree. So let's look at the first one.

EDUCATION AND QUALIFICATIONS

University of Birmingham BSc (Hons.) Computer Science 2013 – Present Day

Subjects include:
Introduction to Nature Inspired Computation; Software Engineering and Computer Vision and Natural Language Technologies.

Now you can, if you wish, go a little bit deeper than this, and the below is a great example of this.

This person has completed a Biomedical Science degree and they have included not only the subjects that they're studying, but the practical skills that they have learned as well. This is most relevant if you want to pursue this subject further, after your studies.

EDUCATION AND QUALIFICATIONS

2011 – 2014 - Northumbria University, Newcastle – Biomedical Science BSc (Hons.) 2.1

Year 1	Year 2	Year 3
Cell biology & Genetics	Pharmacology	Pathology in Practice
Principles of Immunology	Biology of Disease	Clinical Immunology
Introduction of Pathological Sciences	Cellular Pathology	Research Project
Practical Skills of Bioscience	Infection and Immunity	Scientific Literature Review
Applied Anatomy & Physiology	Metabolic Biochemistry	Advanced Immunology
Professional Skills	Medical Microbiology	Biochemistry

Practical skills gained during my degree:

- Practical experience of handling and examining non-pathogenic bacteria in the laboratory
- Laboratory skills (e.g. microscopy, enzymology and quantitative microbiology)

- Practical experience of culturing mammalian cells and of immunological methods
- Practical techniques used to investigate, monitor and treat a specified disease, pathology discipline and evidence knowledge of the disease process itself
- Practical experience in biosensors, spectroscopy (e.g. nuclear magnetic resonance, mass spectroscopy, flow cytometry), separation techniques (e.g. capillary electrophoresis, 2 dimensional electrophoresis, advanced chromatographic separations) and advanced molecular genetics techniques, together with their biomedical applications
- Practical laboratory research of the immune responses in infections, allergies, tumours, immunodeficiency states and autoimmune disorders

This person has studied Biomedical Science and they've included the subjects they've studied during years one, two and three. Now, let me be very clear to you: if you are currently only in year one - you can't put subjects on your CV that you have not yet studied, so you can't include year two or year three subjects. Your CV is written in present day context and so you cannot include things that are likely to happen in the future.

Following on from this, I love the fact that they've also included their practical skills that have been gained during that degree. This is really useful and particularly relevant if you are thinking of working in the same field as your degree. If you studied for example Classics, which you aren't intending to follow up with as a career, then you probably don't need to go into this amount of detail, but if you can, I would say do.

What is a reference?

Moving on to references; what do I mean by references? A reference is written by somebody who can vouch for you, your skills, qualities and experience, but they cannot be personally related.

Most employers generally request two references, often one will be from a previous employer i.e. your manager or, if you have not had a full-time job before, perhaps a lecturer or tutor. The second is often a character reference which can be supplied by somebody that has known you for more than five years, but again do not use somebody that is related to you.

How to include a reference in your CV

To save room on their CVs, most people generally just write 'References available on request'. However, always keep in mind that you will need references for any job, so make sure that you have a plan in your head who to ask when the time comes. If you do choose to name the referees on your CV, you will also need to include their address, contact details, job title and out of courtesy, make sure that you let them know if you will be publishing their personal details on your CV.

Hobbies & Interests also known as Additional Interests and how to include this in your CV

Moving on to hobbies and interests; we could call this 'Additional Information' on a CV, it's really up to you.

I need you to again use some common sense when you come to compiling this section of your CV, *this section* - perhaps more so than any of the others! Now I'm probably being a little bit sarcastic here, but I have to make this point; writing that you frequent the local strip joint is really not going to work! I know that you will

understand this – it's a little bit obvious why it would not work…
but I am going to give you another two examples that won't work
either!

I enjoy a good Western and I also like Twilight (I hate to admit
this). Now, I've most probably watched every single one of them,
but I'm really not going to mention that on my CV!

Some say that you should try and pick hobbies and interests that
highlight transferable skills to the workplace. So for example if
you play a sport, you may want to mention this to associate your
discipline, commitment and ability to work as a team player. Some
people don't always agree with adding personal hobbies and
interests. However, from my point of view, looking at people's
personal hobbies and interests can often give you more of an
insight into a person and how they will fit in with the company
culture. However, what I will say is, don't include the generic
terms such as, "I like reading, socialising or going to the cinema"
as it's well…let's be honest the norm. So if this is all you've got to
say, just leave it out altogether. Think very carefully about what
you include and try to pick selective interests which don't include
Twilight!

Leave out any religion or political parties that you support or
belong to, unless it's obviously job-related.

Task 1 - Joining your CV together

So to summarise, the final part of your CV is adding your
'Additional Information' section by making the most out of your
training and educational achievements as well as thinking about
which of those 'Hobbies and Interests' you're going to include.

So now it's your turn. I would like you to start compiling this
section by digging out your university course handbook and

writing/typing out which modules you've been studying during your first year and the following years (only if relevant to you), and working out which of these modules if any, are relevant to the position that you're applying for.

Here are some additional things that you may also want to consider:

- If your university is impressive, along the lines of Oxford and Cambridge, you may want to highlight this early on in your CV.
- Are you going to showcase the modules you are studying as part of your degree? This is particularly relevant if the course is related to a career that you would like to pursue in the future?
- Are your grades – well... good? If so, highlight this on your CV, if not we can miss them out for now.
- Just something which is obvious, but I see people making this mistake a lot; DO NOT ADD courses/ modules you have not yet completed. So if you're in Year 1, you should not be listing modules that you will be taking in Year 2, for example!
- Do add the dates that you completed courses or if you're still studying, write (for example),
  September 2014 to Present Date.
- Is your CV nicely aligned, i.e. does it look neat and easy to read?
- Don't forget to add at the end. 'References available on request'

Step 7 - The final review...

How to check your CV & we are not just talking spelling or grammatical errors

This is the final step, and we're going to look at how we're going to approach the final review. Stay with me, because this is not just about checking your CV for spelling and grammatical mistakes. We are also going to be looking at how you create a strategy to ensure that your CV is actually seen by the right people and therefore land you that dream job.

So just to recap on what we covered in Step 6. We know that training and education doesn't just cover the formal training that you received in school or college; it also includes in-house training, online courses or it could include something that you've taught yourself.

When we talk about hobbies and interests (additional information), we're don't disclose information that doesn't sell ourselves. We need to be making sure that we're giving the right impression for the job that we want.

We also talked about references and that in order to free up some space on our CV, we can simply just say 'References available on request'.

Finally, what we have learnt throughout this challenge is how to get into that employer mind- set. It has been drilled into you from the first Step to keep thinking, "Is my CV relevant to the position that I'm applying for?"; "Does my CV allow any employer to be able to find out more information about me, should they want to?"; "Does it direct them to where they can go and find that additional information, whether it be my LinkedIn profile, my personal website, blog or portfolio?". You need to ask yourself – does your CV do all of these things?

So back to the final review. After checking for typos and grammatical mistakes, I'd like you to take a day away from your CV, leave it and then come back to it with a fresh pair of eyes. You're likely to think of things in the interim that you would like to add, and additionally, when you come back to it after a break, you may notice things that aren't right.

It is also worth giving your CV to somebody within your chosen profession to get some feedback and perspective on your CV. This is really important, but if you can't find somebody from that particular field, any professional person will be able to help you.

Think again about what we discussed in Step 4 with regard to having different formats available of your CV. So for example, although there are pros to being able to email a pdf of your CV; if your CV is heavily formatted, it is probably not best suited to uploading to a job site. Also, if you need to send your CV via the post – any clickable links will not work, so any website links will need to be written out in full.

How to create a strategy to get you HIRED

Now one thing that I will say and I have found this to be a common problem; many people assume they only need to send their CV to a couple of people, or only apply for a small number of jobs. I don't want you to fall for this misconstrued assumption, as applying for jobs really is a numbers game. Although we have dramatically increased your chances of getting an interview by making your CV very targeted and designing and structuring it well, you are still unlikely to get the first job that you interview for, purely due to the number of people applying for each position these days. The internet has given more people access to jobs that are being advertised and now with modern technology, you can apply for positions from wherever you are in the world – substantially increasing competition for every vacancy. So to beat these odds, it makes sense that the more people you apply to, the more successful you're likely to be. However, I will give you a tip, (its pure common sense really), but you MUST follow up after sending your CV out. It's a good idea, perhaps a week or so later, to give that person a call, or even that job recruitment agency, just to confirm that they have actually received your CV and if they know when interviews will be held. You would be amazed at the number of people that don't do this and actually by following up, you are showing that you are genuinely interested and committed to this particular vacancy.

Additionally, there may be companies that you would be interested in working for but are not actively recruiting currently. It is still worth giving their HR department a call and asking them if you could forward them your CV, just in case anything suitable should crop up in the near future. They will be impressed with your enthusiasm, "Go Get 'Em!" attitude' and ability to be proactive.

Chris Eccles from E4S suggests that you go to this website where you will find a whole range of student jobs, internships, seasonal work, and graduate jobs, as well as extensive advice and industry news. Browse industry insights to pick out jobs that you are best suited to, and then apply for them online. Here are 7 ways to use job boards such as www.e4s.co.uk to land a job:

1. Match your skills with relevant vacancies. Read industry insights and associated job descriptions to see which jobs in which industries match your skills, career aspirations, interests and desired work life balance.

2. Set-up job alerts. Let the job board do the hard work by sifting through vacancies and only emailing you the ones you are interested in.

3. Tailor your CV. Once you know what kind of roles you want to apply for, tweak your CV to highlight the skills and experience which are relevant to those roles.

4. Upload your CV. Let employers find you by uploading your CV to job boards where employers can run searches and contact you with relevant job opportunities.

5. Write a cover letter. For those employers who do not use an application form and ask for a CV, always write a cover letter which summarises your suitability for the job advertised, otherwise your CV may not even be opened.

6. Be specific with your answers to questions. Whether it is on an application form, at interview, or on an assessment day, try to provide specific examples of situations where you have demonstrated key skills and competencies such as teamwork, initiative, good communication, and focus on the positive impact your actions had.

7. Practice. It does make perfect, so practice interview technique via mock interviews as well as the numerical and reasoning tests commonly used at assessment days (https://www.assessmentday.co.uk/buy/aptitudetest_buy.htm).

To land a job you need to convince an employer that you are the best person for their role, so use these 7 steps to sell yourself to them and give yourself the best possible chance of landing your ideal job.

So, create a strategy, it's really important. You need to create plan for which people or companies you are going to send your CV to. So if you send your CV out to 15 different establishments in one week, you need to be following up with calls to all of them the week after. If you think you need a little extra support with this, check out my webinar (fancy name for a video online), 'How to get a job in a day' (http://susanburkecareers.co.uk/shop/how-to-get-a-job-in-a-day)

Why the Follow Up and Follow Through is the key to your success

As part of your CV, you will need to have a cover letter explaining why you believe that you are suitable for the advertised role and the relevant skills, qualities and experience that you have relating to the role (quantifying as on your CV). At the bottom of the cover letter, you would need to include something along the lines of: "I will contact you in the next week or so to ensure that you have received my CV and to find out the next steps". Make sure that you always record who you've spoken to and on what date. Trust me, it is really important that you do this as once you start sending your CV out to lots of different companies, it will all become a blur! Additionally, if you've said that you're going to call somebody at a particular time or day, make sure you do. I call this the FOLLOW THROUGH!

Make sure that you keep your promise, whatever you do, as you need them to know that you are reliable and true to your word. If the person doesn't pick up your call, follow up with an email saying, "As promised, I gave you a call today, but unfortunately you were busy so I will try you again tomorrow", or something along those lines. Make sure that they know that you've gone the extra mile to do this. Trust me, it really does work!

Follow up and follow through, this is again where many, many people let themselves down. If you don't follow up on the CVs that you've sent out, the rest is a waste of time. The FOLLOW THROUGH, although a little scary, is so, so important. Don't get scared and sabotage all of the hard work that you've done so far – these recruiters and hiring managers are all human beings and really nothing to be afraid of. There is a phrase that you should take heed of at this point: 'FEEL THE FEAR, AND DO IT ANYWAY. Who knows what opportunities are lying at the end of that phone call! If you don't get the success you want, dust yourself off and phone the next company and the next, as I promise you that this technique does work, but it takes some guts following this through and this is exactly why some people just won't be able to do it, but not you. You can do it, because by now your CV is so good, you want it to 'Get Noticed and you want to Get Hired!'

You should continue to send out your CV to selected companies and individuals on a weekly basis until you start receiving interviews. Don't stop applying for jobs just because you receive one interview, as you may not actually get the job; so it's best to keep your options open until you have several interviews lined up.

That is the end of Be YOU, Get Noticed, Get Hired, Graduate CV and by now you should have a stunning and professional CV! So please start sending it out straight away and I really would love to hear your success stories; so please email me personally at email@susanburkecareers.co.uk.

Conclusion

II hope you found the book useful, it has really been my honour to have worked with you. If I have managed to make you think and get your CV to a point where it gets you hired, I've done my bit but more importantly, you have done yours. You see sometimes we underestimate things, many people may buy this book, few will put what has been said into practice and I just want to make sure that, that someone is YOU.

You deserve the best and YOU deserve to live life on your terms,

Always Sue ☺

FREE Creative CV Template - As promised if you purchased this book. https://sueburkecareers.leadpages.net/creative-cv

Sign up to my website – come and say Hi, I would love to see you at:

www.susanburkecareers.com

FREE Private Facebook group – Come and join students and graduates from all over the world to get extra tips and support from me personally!
http://j.mp/7DayCVResumeChallenge

If you're a graduate or student you may also be interested in my other book, which is due to, be published in February 2015 'Is your degree worth it? Learn the secrets of successful graduates...'
http://j.mp/mydegreeworthit

You can register to get this book for FREE before this date!
http://j.mp/mydegreeworthit

I would love some help...

My final note is just to say that I really do need reviews for my books to have a chance of standing out from all the books on Amazon, so please do take a couple of minutes to give me some honest feedback which I do hope will be positive, and to let others know how I've managed to help you to stand out from the crowd!

Thank you so much and remember…

Live Life on your terms…

Sue ☺

Appendix 1 - The core Framework for a killer CV!

Name & contact details

Name

Address

Email – think professional email address, nothing silly like Lovemyself@gmail.com or sexycarly@hotmail.com

Mobile, Landline – check correct & make sure the voice message is applicable!

Get them interested in you!

Want to find out more about me?

LinkedIn profile, Twitter, Online portfolio, Website if applicable.

Personal profile

Wow factor…. (anything you write on your CV needs to be backed up with evidence, so don't just use your standard cliché phrases such as teamwork, hard-working, attention to detail etc…). You can use those phrases BUT, they must be backed up with how, what and why you have those skills and qualities and make them highly targeted to the job.

See some examples below (these are purely examples, so don't use them unless you actually have the skills and they are key to the role that you are applying for – this includes any other examples throughout this document).

"I have consistently worked to develop my managerial expertise. For example, whilst working at *Costa Coffee,* I gained a proven track record in increasing sales and turnover (I achieved both green

Win Cards for both stores) and through training and motivation; I inspired the rest of the team to do likewise and in many cases exceed their sales targets".

"I have a proven aptitude for figures as during my most recent role at *Costa Coffee,* I regularly analysed store sales figures and Profit & Loss reports, while also managing and forecasting the budget and was praised for my accurate work and attention to detail."

Yes it is OK to mention it below again if you need to, (remember your profile is just a brief overview, so you can use the 'Skills & Qualities' section below to expand and provide more detail).

Skills & qualities

Skills and qualities must be matched to the job you are applying for), so for example, customer service would be an ideal quality for a position as a Retail Assistant. However, advanced computer skills are probably less relevant, although experience of using different types of electronic tills for example, would definitely be seen as an advantage.

So don't be tempted to list every single skill you can think of.

Think about which skills they have listed in the job description for the role, then think about which of those skills you have, how you have gained them and how you could apply them to what is required in the new role.

Use a MAX of 4 examples.

Qualifications

University degree (particularly if it is relevant to your chosen career), then please expand on the qualifications that you've earned so far and what you're currently studying:

Start with the most recent, including address/full postcode of school/college/Uni

It is ok to include something that you are currently studying, but have not yet finished the course, but don't include something you plan to do in the future – think present day, in fact this goes with anything you include on your CV!

Work History

Work Experience Volunteering

Start with your most recent employment and then work backwards. Provide a sentence on what the company does i.e. *'An online retailer specialising in gifts for under £10'*, and then perhaps you could include a couple of sentences of what your general duties included, and key achievements. You could also list your key achievements as bullet points to keep it clear, concise and easy to read. Remember, recruiters have to read through hundreds of CVs so the clearer yours is the better and if possible quantify it, for example, I reduced costs by 10% or increased sales by 20%.

For example:

2008 - Present, Store Manager, *Costa Coffee, 31 High Street, Wimbledon, SW19*

Costa Coffee is a British multinational coffeehouse company headquartered in Dunstable, United Kingdom, and a wholly owned subsidiary of *Whitbread. My role is the daily management of the store, providing high quality service and managing a team of 20 staff.*

Key Achievements

- Increasing sales by 10% by analysing store figures and improving customer service as well as managing and motivating the team to increase sales and ensure store efficiency.

- Reducing stock, waste and other store costs by 5% resulting in a saving of £10,000 per annum.
- Being able to motivate staff, reduce absenteeism by listening to my staff to improve working conditions.
- Responsible for recruitment and team training provision to help new staff and more experienced staff excel.
- Highly competent to organise work schedules, track accounting and payroll as well provide quarterly reports to the Regional Director.

Additional training

You may have completed a customer care course, first aid, health & safety training or completed in house training for an organisation, well guess what you can mention any of these and even more so if it's relevant!

Awards

As it says on the tin but we are not talking about your 1 metre swimming certificate here!

Professional Associations

Now if you're a little confused about what this is (depending on the type of job you're looking for) you may want to look at some professional associations and see what they are all about, especially if you are studying law, accountancy, surveying etc. Many offer really excellent student rates and some may even be free. They are also great for networking events and getting to know other people/companies within the industry so for the UK it would be http://www.totalprofessions.com/profession-finder and http://fisss.org/sector-skills-council-body and if relevant you could mention this on your CV if you're a member!

Language Skills

If you can speak another language most definitely make them aware of this on your CV!

Testimonial

Who could vouch for you (not always necessary), but if you could include a small paragraph from somebody (an academic tutor, previous employer, somewhere you have volunteered for example), this makes a great sidebar and evidences the skills and talents that you've already stated that you have.

Remember your CV should be no more than 2 pages!

CPSIA information can be obtained at www.ICGtesting.com
Printed in the USA
LVOW04s1254240315

431803LV00001B/310/P

9 781507 609019